D0744260

Kids Making Money

An introduction to financial literacy

by Mattie Reynolds

RED
CHAIR
•PRESS•

Please visit our website at **www.redchairpress.com**.

Find a free catalog of all our high-quality products for young readers.

Kids Making Money

Publisher's Cataloging-In-Publication Data
(Prepared by The Donohue Group, Inc.)

Reynolds, Mattie.
Kids making money : an introduction to financial literacy / by Mattie Reynolds.
p. : col. ill. ; cm. -- (Start smart: money)
Issued also as an ebook.
Summary: Learn about age-appropriate jobs that kids can do. This book will teach you words and ideas about earning money.
Interest age group: 004-008.
Includes bibliographical references and index.
ISBN: 978-1-937529-41-3 (hardcover)
ISBN: 978-1-937529-37-6 (pbk.)
1. Money-making projects for children--Juvenile literature. 2. Children--Employment--Juvenile literature. 3. Children--Finance, Personal--Juvenile literature. 4. Moneymaking projects. 5. Children--Employment. 6. Finance, Personal. I. Title.
HF5392 .R49 2013

650.1/2/083   2012943324

Photo credits:
© Ariel Skelley/CORBIS: front cover, 1, 12
Dreamstime: pages 5, 7, 13, 20, back cover
iStockphoto LP: pages 8, 9, 21
Shutterstock Images LLC: 3, 6, 11, 14, 15, 17, 18, 19

Reading specialist: Linda Cornwell, Literacy Connections Consulting

This edition first published in 2013 by

Red Chair Press LLC   PO Box 333   South Egremont, MA 01258-0333

Printed in The United States of America

1 2 3 4 5 17 16 15 14 13

Table of Contents

Words in **bold type** are defined in the glossary.

CHAPTER 1

Why People Earn Money

People **earn** money for many reasons. People earn money to buy things they need for their family. A family needs a place to live. A family needs food and clothes.

People also earn money to buy things they want. Someone might want to buy tickets to a movie. Another person might want to buy popcorn. People earn money to buy things they need and things they want.

People earn money for things they want.

A person earns money by working at a **job**. Some jobs can be done in a few hours or days. At the end of the job, the person is paid for the work done.

Other jobs are done every day. Some jobs are done outside. People may work on farms outside. Sometimes people who build houses work outside.

There are jobs that can be done inside, too. A person may go to a store or to an office to do the work. If someone likes to talk to people, they may choose to work as a salesperson in a store.

For some jobs, a person may go to school a long time. It takes special skills to be a doctor or teacher. But for each job, the person earns money. Then they can buy what they need and some things they want.

CHAPTER 2

Jobs Kids Can Do

Many jobs must be done by a grown-up person. Only an adult can be a police officer or dentist. But are there jobs kids can do? Yes! There are lots of jobs for kids.

To decide what job may be right, kids might ask themselves these questions.
Do I like to be inside or outside?
Do I like animals?
Am I good at talking to adults?

There are many jobs kids can do.

Jaden likes animals. His grandmother has a dog named Oscar. Jaden offers to wash Oscar once a week. His grandmother agrees to pay Jaden one dollar each time. Jaden and Oscar both like this job!

Emily enjoys being outside. Her mother does not have time to take care of the garden. Now Emily is paid two dollars for each hour that she weeds and waters the garden. If Emily wants to earn $8 to go to a movie, she knows she must work four hours to earn the money.

$$\$2 \times 4 \text{ hours} = \$8$$

Kayla has a job inside. Her parents both work and are very busy. Kayla helps by folding clothes from the dryer. Kayla helps her younger sister pick out her clothes for school each day. And she teaches her sister to make her bed. For these jobs, Kayla gets paid an **allowance** each week.

Micah likes his neighbor, Mrs. Simmons. She makes the best oatmeal cookies! Mrs. Simmons sells her cookies at the local market. She earns $3 for each bag. Micah helps Mrs. Simmons make the cookies and is paid $1 for each bag. Both Micah and Mrs. Simmons have a sweet job!

CHAPTER 3

Using Money You Earn

Now we know some ways adults and kids earn money. When someone works at a job for many weeks and months, the money adds up. So how can money be used?

Money has **value**. Value is how much the money is worth or can buy. Someone might earn $20 at a job. But if that is all the money she has, should she spend it on a video game that costs $20? If she did, she would have no money left.

The coins and bills of money have value.

To earn more money, a person can work longer at a job. The smart way to take care of money is to save. Some people save half their money each time they are paid.

Kevin earns $2 each week raking leaves. Each week, he puts $1 in his money jar. He knows he can spend the rest. Kevin likes watching the money fill up the jar! Kevin saves half of what he earns to buy a new book.

Emily saves part of the allowance she earns each week. She has a piggy bank where she puts money to save. Emily also shares her money. Emily likes giving part of her money to a **charity** her parents helped her find. She knows the money she gives will help other children.

By earning money, kids can buy what they need, save for what they want, and still have money to share with others.

Glossary

allowance: money paid regularly to a child for specific purposes or tasks

charity: an organization that provides help and raises money for people in need

earn: to get paid money in return for labor or services

job: a task or a type of work for which someone is paid

value: what something is worth or what an amount of money can buy

For More Information

Books

Firestone, Mary. *Earning Money* (Learning About Money). Mankato, MN: Capstone Press, 2005.

Hall, Margaret. *Your Allowance* (Earning, Saving, Spending). Chicago, IL: Heinemann, 2008.

Larson, Jennifer S. *What Can You Do with Money?* (Lightning Bolt Books). Minneapolis, MN: Lerner Publishing, 2010.

Orr, Tamra. *A Kid's Guide to Earning Money* (Money Matters). Hockessin, DE: Mitchell Lane, 2009.

Toren, Adam and Matthew Toren. *Kidpreneurs: Young Entrepreneurs with Big Ideas!* Phoenix, AZ: Business Plus Media, 2009.

Web Sites

US Mint: H.I.P. Pocket Change
http://www.usmint.gov/kids/games/

PBS Kids: Be Your Own Boss
http://pbskids.org/itsmylife/games/boss/

TheMint.org: 7 Ways Kids Can Earn Money
http://www.themint.org/kids/ways-kids-can-earn-money.html

The Motley Fool: Kids Earning Money
www.fool.com/foolu/askfoolu/2002/askfoolu021218.htm

Index

About the Author

Mattie Reynolds practices the four basic skills of financial literacy in her life. She earned money in the insurance business and learned to save for things her family needed. Mattie continues to be a smart shopper buying what she needs and saving for what she wants. She shares with her church and charity in Duncan, Oklahoma, where she lives.